AF469250

BASINGSTOKE PAST AND PRESENT

ROBERT BROWN

Published by Ensign Publications
2 Redcar Street, Shirley, Southampton SO1 5LL

ISBN 185455 007 1

Design by Mark Eslick

Typeset by R.A. Design, New Milton, Hampshire.

Jacket front: WINCHESTER STREET 1937. Basingstoke celebrated the Coronation of King George VI in 1937 with the decoration of the streets and buildings in the town. The road on the right was Victoria Street, widened and improved from the original Allen's Lane in 1899. New Street on the left was once known as Stew Lane.

Jacket back: BASINGSTOKE RAILWAY STATION c. 1900. Built in 1839, it was rebuilt in 1897 and 1904. The Railway was opened from London to Basingstoke in June 1839 and from Basingstoke to Southampton in May 1840. The Reading line was opened in 1848. The tracks were electrified in 1964. In 1984 the Booking Office was altered with a general refurbishing, giving the station a smart, modern appearance.

INTRODUCTION

In October 1961 an agreement was signed by the Basingstoke Borough Council, Hampshire County Council, and London County Council, which led to the development and expansion of Basingstoke, in North East Hampshire. The agreement resulted in the demolition of the town centre and the construction of the present shopping area and multi-storey car park. In addition came a completely new arterial road system, the building of some 8,000 dwellings and the development of various industrial and commercial sites around the town. The mammoth task of rebuilding an old town into a new one was a difficult one, most of the services had to be completely renewed, such as water, gas, and electricity mains. The telephone system was replaced, roads were closed and rebuilt, bus routes were altered, even the River Loddon was diverted.

The demolition of the old town centre saw the demise of most of the public houses, many of the little shops, a school, a cinema, restaurants, cafes, and a large number of houses. Farms on the outskirts of the town were acquired by compulsory purchase such as Buckskin, Chineham, South Ham, and West Ham, to allow housing and industrial estates to be built. In the following years some 400 firms moved into Basingstoke, under the Town Development Scheme, which brought both employers and employees from London and elsewhere. A Development Group was formed, with an office in the town, from where a Director and a team of planners controlled the vast operation in the years between 1961 and 1977.

To local folk the collective memory of the early days of the Town Development consist mostly of smoke and dust as each road in the town centre was methodically demolished and levelled. Then came the arrival of the pile-drivers and the constant "thump thump" as they operated day after day during those winter months of 1967. It seemed as if they would never stop, but they finally did. Out of all this seeming chaos there emerged a bright new town with modern shops, new factories and offices, and an orbital road around it all.

But what of the old town, with many of its buildings dating back hundreds of years, sadly they were gone, but certainly not forgotten. A unique photographic record was kept of nearly every building in the area, over the years a whole series of books and other publications have been published as an illustrated record of how Basingstoke looked before all the changes took place. Even now, with the arrival of more newcomers to the town and given the enquiring minds of young people who are growing up in the area, there is still a great need for further detailed information of how the town used to look. There is doubt in some people's minds as to where certain places were in comparison with today's buildings and streets.

Many people may not realise that the shopping precinct Potters Walk is on the site of Potters Lane where there used to be a line of small shops specialising in a variety of individual trades. The confectionery and bakers shop kept by Ruby and Winifred Philpott had a mocked-up wedding cake in the shop window originally crafted by their father in 1898. It was finally removed when the shop closed in September 1964. Further down the street was the bicycle shop of Mr. Everett—Charlie to everyone—where the folk took their trusty "steeds" for repair. He would lift them up onto his "meat-hooks" which hung from the ceiling, and carry out the repair without ever having to bend down.

The Shopping Centre now caters for many similar requirements, the street names at least are preserved in the titles of the precincts. Another name is St. John's Walk, which comes from the Church of England school that stood at the bottom of Church Street. Built in 1901 the school was constructed on the site of an old farm, which in turn was the place where Walter de Merton's hospice for elderly priests used to stand in the 14th century. Not far away, on a site now undermined by the Churchill Way "tunnel" stood the Fire Station, originally built in 1913, where hundreds of children over the years must have stood watching the fire engines turning out to fight the many fires that Basingstoke suffered in the years up to 1966.

Further afield, at Winklebury, who would imagine that the area once housed a grim collection of little shanty-type homes spread along ancient tracks which probably dated back to the Romans who built their Silchester to Winchester road very close to here. How many people realise that the fields near Five-ways at Kempshott was the site of a race-course in the 18th and 19th centuries; and just a mile away at Worting village there stood a large tyre-retread factory, which existed between 1926 and 1974.

To the many who are new to the area these vital snippets of information can be of great interest, they will add depth to their view of the new town. After all, most folk like to know a little of the history of their chosen domicile, even if it is only their immediate home area. It is always interesting to compare a picture taken many years ago with an up-to-date scene, in this book, Basingstoke Past and Present, we have set out simply to do just that. Some of the old views have buildings which are still there, some have not a single thing to go by, such as in the New Shopping Area. Most of these pictures feature scenes which include at least one clue as to where they are now, the reader is invited to enquire within! It is hoped that many people, young and old, newcomers and long time residents, will enjoy touring the town with this volume in their pockets, exploring the reality of the present with the help of scenes from the past.

Robert Brown
Basingstoke 1988

CONTENTS

HACKWOOD ROAD 1960. This row of shops and offices stood where the present Civic Offices are. Raymond Dudman kept his general stores there, while further along Nancy Noyes' bookshop attracted the many book lovers of the town. In between there was a builder's office and yard owned by Mr. A. J. Sapp. All were cleared to allow the construction of the Council Offices in 1975.

HACKWOOD ROAD 1988. Now called New Road, which curves round to Victoria Street and Giffords Corner, this scene shows part of the Civic Offices with the War Memorial Park trees in the background. Many of these were blown down in the storm of October last year, during which the Park lost 30 fine trees.

NEW STREET 1930. The old building behind the tree was demolished in 1933 to make way for a parade of shops, while the road was widened at that point. Some of the early traders of that time remained there until recent years, such as Kenneth Reed, the Chemist, and Bateson and Nicholas, the estate agents. The cottages on the right were later converted into shops.

NEW STREET 1988. Where the road used to bend into Cross Street and Flaxfield Road it now dips down into Timberlake Road, while Queen's Parade has been left high and dry above the road. In the background is the National Farmers' Union offices, which has grown from its original Cross Street office of previous years.

THE BASINGSTOKE TOWN HALL 1910. The clock tower, erected in 1887 by the local benefactor and Mayor of Basingstoke, John May, replaced a smaller structure built with the Town Hall in 1832. This taller tower became unsafe in later years and was dismantled in 1961. The lamp in the Market Place was erected in 1903 in memory of the May family, who had brought much prosperity and good cheer into the town through their large brewery in Brook Street.

THE BASINGSTOKE TOWN HALL 1988. The Town Hall clock tower, erected at the expense of John May, the local benefactor, in 1887, was dismantled in 1961. The shop to the right of the Town Hall, previously Mr. Buckland's stationery store, was W. H. Smith's bookshop between 1934 and 1970, until they moved down to the New Shopping Centre.

THE GOLDINGS ESTATE 1920. This private estate, situated between Hackwood Road and London Road, was acquired by two local businessmen in 1901 as a Park for the town. Named the Basingstoke War Memorial Park, in memory of those who died during the Great War, it was laid out at the expense of £4,496, while the mansion house was bought for £10,000 for use as municipal buildings for the local council.

THE WAR MEMORIAL PARK 1988. Over the years the Park has been the venue for many events, including the annual Carnival, and for a time the Whitsun Sports Day. With tennis courts, football pitches, a paddling pool, and a bowling green, amongst other facilities, the Park became a favourite place for general recreation. Some of those features have gone in recent years, but the bandstand has been restored to its former glory.

WINCHESTER ROAD c.1900. The left side of the road belonged to the Manor House, the home of John Mares, the rain-coat manufacturer, while the right side was mainly Brinkletts Farm, the wall and trees obscuring the large farmyard. Brinklets House is in the centre of the picture.

WINCHESTER ROAD 1988. Brinkletts House has had extensive alterations and extensions for conversion into offices in recent years; while the farmyard has been taken over as a car park. Manor House opposite was the offices of the Southern Electricity Board until recently when new offices were built next door.

WINCHESTER STREET c. 1920. The shops on the right were later acquired by the Co-operative Society, while other shops in New Street, round the corner, were also taken over. In 1960 these were demolished and a new Co-op Store was built. The building on the left was the Victoria Hotel, which in later years became a public house.

WINCHESTER STREET 1988. On the right Copenhagen Court offices now replaces the old Co-op Stores which closed down in 1985 and were then demolished. The old Victoria Hotel building opposite was converted into solicitors' offices. But the road itself is no wider, and now presents the town with a bottle-neck for both traffic and pedestrians.

WINCHESTER STREET c. 1900. The building on the right was later demolished and Marks and Spencers built a store there in 1934. Next door was a bank, which in turn became the grocers Mr. Ody, who closed down in 1966. Opposite was the entrance into Mr. Joice's yard, where he made and repaired coaches and other horse carriages.

WINCHESTER STREET 1988. Mr. Ody's grocery is now the Halifax building society offices; Marks and Spencers moved down to the New Shopping Centre, allowing various firms to move in until the building was gutted by fire in 1984. In the background a completely new set of shops has changed the roofline in the Market Place.

WORTING ROAD c. 1920. Looking towards the town from the Alton Light Railway bridge, the view shows the Cemetery lodge on the right, while on the left is part of the motor manufacturers, Thornycrofts. The Cemetery was opened and dedicated in May, 1913, the 25 acre site costing nearly £3,000 to be laid out. Thornycrofts was established in 1898 and produced many hundreds of vehicles, until it was taken over by Eatons in 1973.

WORTING ROAD 1988. With the exception of a new bridge over the present Ring Road, which the bollard and island belong to, and the growth of the trees on the left, the scene has hardly changed. The Alton Light Railway, built in 1901, closed down in 1932. The Worting Road bridge was demolished and rebuilt for the Ring Road underneath in 1970.

WINTON SQUARE 1910. Mr. Durant's shop contained a variety of goods, from sweets to fancy goods. He had a good supply of books and magazines, and all types of stationery. In later years the building underwent a lot of changes, with the windows being mainly bricked up. During the last War it became the local Food Office.

WINTON SQUARE 1988. Mr. Durant's shop is now an employment agency, the upper part of the building having been hardly altered at all. With the horse trough removed in the 1950's, road traffic moved much easier through the square, but the "keep clear" signs on the road tell a story of present access problems.

WINCHESTER ROAD c. 1915. This view shows the junction of Bramblys Grange, left, with the old Black Horse public house on the right. By then the Inn had been converted into a cottage. It was later demolished to make way for two new houses built further back. Bramblys Grange was a large private estate with a mansion, owned by Mr. Thornycroft, of the local motor vehicle firm.

WINCHESTER ROAD 1988. On the corner stands an office block built by Guardian Royal Exchange, covering some 13,000 square feet, on land that used to belong to the White Garage. Further along the road, on the right-hand side, several old buildings have been replaced, but one building remains—the Manor House, where the Electricity Board had their offices.

UPPER WOTE STREET c. 1920. The main Post Office was established here in 1883 and remained until 1925 when it was moved to new premises in New Street. Opposite, on the right of the picture, was the Emmanuel Church, which was established in 1779, and demolished in 1966.

UPPER WOTE STREET 1988. The old Post Office building remains, now Hammicks Bookshop, but the rest of the scene has changed. The tree on the right is all that is left of the Emmanuel Church grounds, the site of which is now a D.I.Y. shop. The multi-storey car park and the new Churchill Plaza office block is in the background.

THE BASINGSTOKE TOWN HALL AND MARKET PLACE 1830. The Town Hall, on the left, was built in 1657 after a fire destroyed the previous one the year before. In 1832 an Act of Parliament allowed the building to be demolished and a new Town Hall to be erected on the site of the two shops and public house on the right. One shop belonged to Mr. Caston, who moved into premises in an alley opposite.

THE BASINGSTOKE TOWN HALL AND MARKET PLACE 1988. Where the old Town Hall used to stand is now the top of Church Street. The present building ceased to be the Town Hall in October 1981, its function as council offices having ended many years beforehand, when the Civic Offices were built in 1975. Lloyds Bank was built in 1926.

UPPER CHURCH STREET 1910. Typical of many of Basingstoke's roads in those early days, Church Street was quite narrow. The store on the right, The Little Dust Pan, was bought by Mr. William Aston in 1930 who converted it into a drapery arcade, which included among its attractions, an aviary.

UPPER CHURCH STREET 1988. Pedestrianised in July of this year the street is just as busy with shoppers as they make their way from the top of the town to the New Shopping Centre, and vice versa. In the background is the tower of St. Michael's Church while further on the offices of Provident Life can be seen on the hill by the Railway.

WINCHESTER ROAD AREA 1964. This area once held a large complex of greenhouses owned by several firms, upon the Town Development Scheme taking over the land, housing estates were constructed on both sides of the Winchester Road. In the foreground is Pittard Road being built, while in the background the land has been cleared for the Kings Furlong estate.

WINCHESTER ROAD AREA 1988. The Winchester Road houses are mainly hidden from view by the houses built in Pittard and Packenham Roads, while tucked away on the main road the Kings public house, previously the King of Wessex, and several shops, replace a row of council houses which were built in 1914 and demolished in the mid-1950's.

LOWER WOTE STREET 1962. Linked with Reading Road, Brook Street, and Station Hill, this was the hub of activity for both travellers and entertainment seekers. The Bus, Coach and Railway Stations were all close to each other, with the two leading cinemas, the Waldorf and Savoy, just yards away, making this area the "Piccadilly Circus" of Basingstoke. The Waldorf Cinema, on the right, was built in 1935 by George Casey, who owned other cinemas in the town.

LOWER WOTE STREET 1988. Over the 26 years since the previous picture was taken, Jackson's Garage has grown and the Gents toilet, the Hornbeam tree, and horse-trough have gone. The old Waldorf cinema has changed its name to the Cannon. The pillars of the Shopping Centre block out part of the scene this being the entrance into the Churchill Way "tunnel", allowing traffic to reach the other side of the town.

BUCKSKIN FARM 1960. Dating back to the 17th century this farm was to be enveloped by the Town Development Scheme in 1965. After 19 years of farming Cecil Gibbons and his family moved away to Berkshire. Mr. Gibbons' father moved to Buckskin Farm from Old Basing in 1920 and farmed there until he retired in 1946. His son then took over the tenancy of the land, which was owned by Lord Camrose, until he moved away.

BUCKSKIN ESTATE 1988. Previously Buckskin Farm, the land was acquired under the Town Development Scheme of 1961 as one of the town's major housing projects. Buckskin 1 estate contains 348 houses, while the second phase contains 744 houses. The actual Buckskin Farmhouse was kept as a council rent office for some years until it closed down. In among the many houses a group of shops and a public house were built.

FORD BUILDINGS c. 1910. These old cottages were previously the local Workhouse buildings, in Brook Street, but upon new and larger premises being erected in Basing Road in 1836 they were sold to Mr. John Ford, who converted them into separate homes for local people. The road to the left led up to the Cricketers Arms public house, and a flight of steps took people up to the Railway Goods Yard.

FORD BUILDINGS SITE 1988. Now the Victory Roundabout, named after the Victory Inn which stood on the Essex Road side of Brook Street. The Brook House offices took its name from an old mansion house in Brook Street, where the local High School originated from earlier this century. This area used to be known as Noah's Island in the 19th century.

CHAPEL STREET c. 1915. Looking down from the Railway bridge, the old 17th century cottages were to last another fifty years before their walls were torn down for Town Development. Junction Road, to the left, was built in 1871 to allow easier access to the Railway Station from the Newbury road. At the bottom of Chapel Street was Brook street which divided here, the right side passing the Brewery belonging to the May family.

CHAPEL STREET SITE 1988. The modern view from the Railway Station shows a completely different panorama to the old one. The Shopping Centre and multi-storey car park now dominate the skyline. No more will we see the various roof-tops that countless rail travellers used to look down on when passing through Basingstoke.

MARKET PLACE c. 1910. The Old Angel Cafe on the right was once the premises of the Angel Inn, which dated from the 16th century and which closed down in 1866. This extensive building was very popular with stage-coach travellers en route between London and the West Country. In more recent years the building housed Barclays Bank. Bowman's store later became the International Stores.

MARKET PLACE 1988. During the construction of Barclays Bank, in the mid-1920's, some interesting items were found belonging to the old Angel Inn, while in 1928 work on the building next door revealed wallpaper dating back over a hundred years. The Sleep Shop replaced International Stores, which was there for many years.

UPPER CHURCH STREET 1935. This was the scene after the fire of 1935 when Mr. Aston's arcade was gutted. The fire started in combustible material in the centre of the shop, and quickly spread to the rest of the building. The local Fire Brigade had difficulty in containing the fire, an adjoining house was also damaged. Later the road was widened at this point.

UPPER CHURCH STREET 1988. After the 1935 fire a new parade of shops was built with flats above. Also included were offices, known as the Market Chambers, where the Inspector of Taxes and other local departments were situated. The Southern Electricity showrooms were here before they moved down to the New Shopping Centre.

THE HOLY GHOST CHAPEL RUINS, 17th CENTURY. Situated close to the Railway station, on the Chapel Hill side, the Chapel was built in the 15th century, although parts of it originate from the 13th century Holy Ghost Guild. The cottage on the left was a schoolhouse, from whence could be heard the cries of Mrs. Blunden who was buried alive here by accident in 1674

THE HOLY GHOST CHAPEL RUINS 1988. In recent years the gravestones have been removed and used as pathways, while several small trees have been planted obscuring the ruins. Since the 17th century there has been further deterioration in the structure, hastened by both weather and vandals.

THE SLAUGHTER-HOUSE, WOTE STREET 1960. This old building was the end of the journey for many animals sold at the Cattle Market, which was held weekly near the Railway Station. Cattle were herded down Station Hill and up Wote Street to this place ready for the butchers. It was closed down in 1973 and demolished the following year.

FEATHERS LANE 1988. Previously the site of the Slaughter-house, it now houses a row of shops and offices. It also allows people access to the car park behind New Road and London Street, from Upper Wote Street.

WINTON SQUARE 1970. The old horse trough of earlier days was replaced by traffic bollards, while Wilkinsons' fruit shop became a Turf Accountants. The White Garage had access through to the Winchester Road, where it had petrol pumps and a car repair section.

WINTON SQUARE 1988. Although the shops have changed, once again the tops of the buildings have stayed the same. The road bollards have been modernised and the street lamp has changed. The White Garage closed down a few years ago, while the other shops moved out before then.

WORTING VILLAGE 1960. These old cottages were demolished to make way for a wider access into Kempshott Lane, close to the Railway bridge. The house in the background was also used as a general stores called Habberfields, while close by was an old tree that was used in the past as one of the stopping places in the "Beating the Bounds" custom.

WORTING VILLAGE 1988. Now the junction of Kempshott Lane and Worting Road, the site of Habberfield's store holds part of a row of homes and some shops. Opposite this junction there used to be the Tyre Retread factory of Blue Peter, which was established in 1926, it closed down in 1973. The extensive buildings were taken over by various independent firms.

WINCHESTER STREET 1958. The South side of the road has changed considerably over the years, and only one shop has remained the same—Chesterfield's, which was established in 1913 as a men's outfitters. It was in this road that Milwards shoe shop began its expansion all over the country. Marks and Spencers came to Basingstoke in 1934.

WINCHESTER STREET 1988. There is little change in the tops of the shops, but one building is different—that of the Royal Bank of Scotland, to the right. This was previously a furniture shop (originally Marks and Spencers) but a fire gutted the premises in 1984 and the building had to be pulled down. Next to the Bank, the Halifax Building Socciety took over Mr. Ody's grocery shop, after its closure in 1966.

THE ENGINEERS ARMS 1966. Situated on the corner of Reading Road and Basing Road, this public house was named after the nearby engineering firm of Wallis and Steevens, which was built in Station Hill in 1860. Workmen from the factory would use the public house during their dinner break. Just yards away (upper left in the picture) was the Old House at Home pub.

CHURCHILL WAY 1988. Previously the site of Reading Road, hardly anything remains of the old scene. Only the entrance into the Bus Station at the bottom right of the picture is the same. The large office blocks of Alencon Link and Eastrop View dominate the skyline, while Eastrop Roundabout at least gives the scene some greenery.

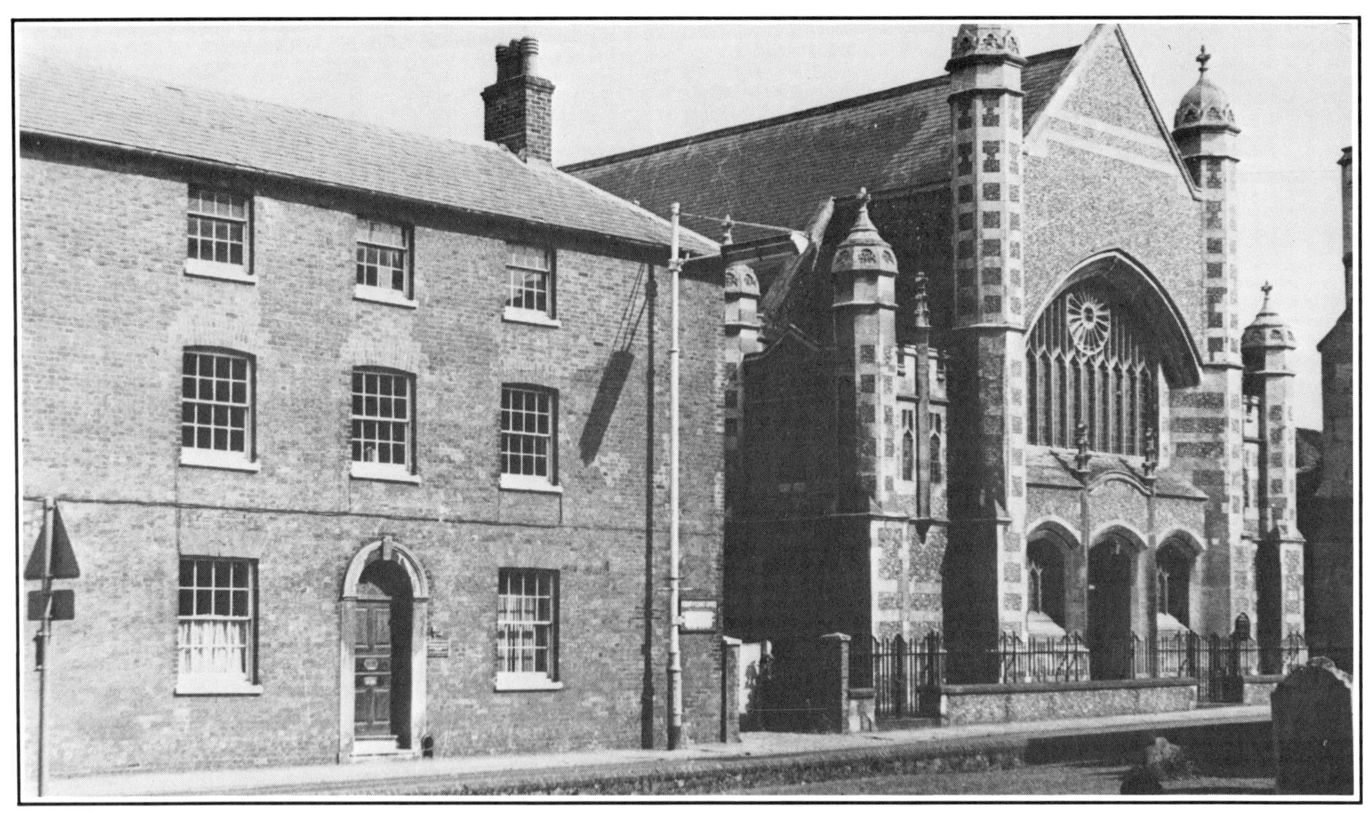

CHURCH STREET METHODIST CHURCH 1966. Built in 1905, to replace a chapel which was moved stone by stone to Cliddesden village, it was badly damaged by a German bomb during the Second World War in 1940. Extensive repairs were carried out and the Church was re-opened for religious services by 1951. The last service was held in October 1965 prior to its demolition for the New Shopping Centre. The building next door was the local County Court offices.

CHURCH STREET METHODIST CHURCH SITE 1988. The slope up to the Shopping Centre contains a plaque recording the fact that the Methodist Church stood on that site. The building to the left of the slope is part of the large Sports Centre which is incorporated into the complex of shops.

WALLIS AND STEVENS, STATION HILL 1967. Established in 1860 this engineering firm began as Wallis and Haslam, then changed its name in later years. Well known for its famous steamrollers and other heavy vehicles, the firm moved up to Daneshill in 1966, then closed down a few years later. The Station Hill site was demolished in 1967.

WALLIS AND STEEVENS SITE 1988. Now part of the New Shopping Centre and Alencon Link, there is nothing to link the scene with the previous picture. This area was completed in the period 1978/79, and now contains Sainsbury's store and other well-known shops. This part of the Shòpping Centre faces the Railway Station, which in recent years has had a general face-lift.

LOWER CHURCH STREET 1966. This part of the road was saved from demolition for the New Shopping Centre, allowing the traders to continue their business. The building on the right dates back to the 17th century, and has some old beams to prove it. At the rear of these shops were the Rectory grounds.

LOWER CHURCH STREET 1988. Due to be partly demolished and developed, these shops have seen a variety of shopkeepers over the years, including an insurance broker, newsagent and turf acccountant. For some years the 17th century building in the distance was converted into a bank, but they moved out several years ago.

LOWER CHURCH STREET 1966. Taken during the Mayoral Parade of 1966, when Cllr. Harold Redstall was Mayor, this shows the part of Church Street which was severed by Timberlake Road in later years. The building on the left was Bedford House, with its prominent porch, while in the background was the Conservative Club, which opened in 1909 and moved to Bounty Road in 1966.

LOWER CHURCH STREET 1988. A high wall replaces the previous scene, behind which is the New Shopping Centre. The bridge on the right spans Timberlake Road, which cuts through the Centre like a tunnel. Built in the period 1967-68, this became phase one of a vast project.

CHAPEL STREET 1960. These old 17th century cottages were situated just below the Railway bridge, a classic example of timbered buildings of that period. They were demolished, along with their wattle and mud walls, in 1967, to allow the road to be widened. To the left of the cottages was the entrance into the Railway Goods Yard, which no longer exists.

CHAPEL STREET SITE 1988. Now cleared of buildings, the area is now the junction of Provident Way and Chapel Hill. The road on the left leads up to the offices of Provident Life, while the Railway is in the background.

LOWER WOTE STREET 1963. This scene faced Goat Lane, with its famous 17th century public house The Goat. The alleyway on the far left was Bedford Place, which led through to Church Street, in which two rows of terraced houses stood. Watson's Garage moved up to London Road when the area was taken over for demolition for the New Shopping Centre.

LOWER WOTE STREET SITE 1988. The New Market Square now covers the area of the previous picture. The Goat Inn was demolished in mid-1965 with other buildings in the road, to make way for the New Market Square shops, built to house traders who lost their shops in the lower part of the town the following year.

BUNNIAN PLACE 1963. This short road, which led from the Railway down to the Reading Road, once had six public houses in it. Now only the Queen's Arms remains, at the top of the hill. All the other buildings in the road were demolished to make way for the Town Development Scheme. The road was named after an old gate that used to stand at the junction of Clifton Way, which was originally called "Bunny's Bar".

BUNNIAN PLACE 1988. Looking like a scene from Dallas, the road has changed out of all character to how it used to be. The view looking south to the I.B.M. building and beyond to the Churchill Plaza offices by the Bus Station, gives a good idea of how the town has become commercialised over the years.

LONDON STREET c. 1960. One of the many annual Carnival parades passing through the centre of the town. In the background can be seen Webber's Garage, which later moved to New Road; Currys electrical shop, now in the Shopping Centre; and Woolworths, also in the Centre. The Carnivals were first established in the 1930's, then revived in 1956, and held every year since.

LONDON STREET 1988. Webber's Garage has been changed into two shop units; Currys shop is now a double-glazing shop; and Woolworths is now the Main Post Office. The Carnival processions no longer go though London Street, as it is now pedestrianised.

WINCHESTER ROAD 1962. This was the junction of Winchester Road and the Basingstoke By-Pass, which was quite often the scene of road accidents similar to this one. The By-Pass, built in 1931, took most of the traffic away from the town, and at holiday times there was one long line of vehicles stretching for miles past this point. The construction of the M3 motorway in 1970 relieved the situation considerably.

WINCHESTER ROAD 1988. Road widening and a large roundabout has brought the accident rate down at this point. In the background is Smith's Industries factory, which when first opened in 1937 was Kelvin, Bottomley and Baird, one of the first firms to be established along the Winchester Road.

THE CATTLE MARKET 1966. This was the scene after the Market closed down in May 1966. Situated off Clifton Terrace, near the Railway Station, the Cattle Market was established in 1873 by Mr. Hugh Raynbird and his two sons. Over the following years the area was extended to include offices, auction rings, stables and sheds to house a wide variety of animals.

THE CATTLE MARKET SITE 1988. Now an attractive garden area by the Alencon Link subway, the place now has no resemblance to its previous appearance. Hidden behind the trees is Clifton House offices named after Clifton Terrace, where the Cattle Market used to be held. In the background is the tall office block of I.B.M. in Bunnian Place, one of several buildings that the firm has acquired.

LOWER BROOK STREET 1966. Looking towards the town, this view shows the rear of May Street houses (left) and the builders yard of W.W. Hall. May Street was demolished to make way for the Churchill Way West dual carriageway, while the land on the right was cleared for a private housing development. The far end of the road was a location for the filming of George Formby's comedy "He Snoops to Conquer" in 1944.

LOWER BROOK STREET 1988. On the left is the Brookvale Association community hall, while in the background are the offices in Alencon Link. In early November every year the Brookvale people gather on the green at the end of the road for the annual firework display and bonfire.

HACKWOOD ROAD 1960. It was originally known as Duke Street, as it led to the Duke of Bolton's estate at Hackwood Park. To the left there used to be a garden nursery, while opposite a row of picturesque thatched cottages gave the road much charm. Further down the road, on the right, was the Horse and Jockey public house, which had associations with the Kempshott horse racing in the 18th and 19th centuries.

HACKWOOD ROAD 1988. The demolition of a row of houses and a public house, with road widening, has made this part of Basingstoke another changed place. The Cottage Hospital, hidden round the corner, opened in 1879, is still in use but does not deal with casualty and other urgent hospital services, which are now dealt with at the main hospital off Aldermaston Road.

FLAXFIELD ROAD 1967. This building housed the shop, office, and residence of Thorntons Bakery, which was established by Henry Thornton in 1886. The yard behind housed the bakery and ovens. As the business expanded so Mr. Thornton opened up other shops in the town, some with cafes attached. The business closed down in 1967.

FLAXFIELD ROAD 1988. The bakery has been replaced, being demolished in 1968, with a forecourt and tyre repair service building. In the background are new offices recently built in Essex Road.

SOUTH HAM FARM 1960. Once the home of farmer John Bennett the farm land was acquired to build one of Basingstoke's largest council house estates for the Town Development Scheme of 1961. But even before then various parts of the farm had been purchased, first in 1900 for the building of the Alton Light Railway, then later to erect some 270 houses between 1931 and 1938. In 1952 further land was taken for the construction of Western Way and other roads.

RUSSELL HOWARD PARK. Previously the South Ham farmland, this area was preserved for recreation purposes and named after a well known local Councillor and Mayor. Laid out in 1967, the avenue of trees, where flights of birds carry out their nightly ritual before settling down into their roosts, were retained as a natural feature. A childrens playground, bowling greens, football pitches, and a cricket ground were all incorporated into the Park.

LONDON STREET c. 1900. In the distance, on the left, is the Red Lion Hotel which was a popular coaching Inn in the 18th century. It was originally a two storey building, but has been expanded over the years. Opposite was Mark Lane with its Forge and Smithy, and the workshops of Thomas Burberry, the raincoat manufacturer. In 1888 the local Police Station was built there, before it moved to London Road in 1967.

LONDON STREET 1988. Although there have been several changes over the years, the Westminster Bank, now the National Westminster, stands out on the left of the picture. Next to it is the Main Post Office, which moved to that site from New Street in 1971. Opposite was Boots the Chemist, now the Midland Bank.

CHURCH SQUARE c. 1910. The scene of many gatherings and parades, this square is the main entrance into St. Michael's Church, the Parish church. This scene is of a Mayor's Parade earlier this century, when various local military and other groups assembled prior to giving thanks in the form of a service in the church. The houses in the background were badly damaged by German bombs in August 1940, when many local folk were killed.

CHURCH SQUARE 1988. Since the bombing raid of 1940 the area has been laid out as a garden of remembrance, with the addition of bungalows for retired people. This was done during the mid-1950's, when a similar garden for the blind was laid out on the corner of the Square and Mortimer Lane.

UPPER CHURCH STREET c. 1900 A typical scene in the early years of this century. The men are standing outside the Black Boy Hotel, which in later years beame the present Hop Leaf public house. The next building down was the Eagle Inn, which closed down at the end of the 19th century. The stone eagles on the roof were later removed to top the Black Boy Hotel.

UPPER CHURCH STREET 1988. The Hop Leaf public house gets a face-lift after many years, the left-hand window is of a similar design to its ancient predecessor. Previously known as the Black Boy Hotel its name was changed about 30 years ago. Griffin's butcher shop has retained its old frontage, although the shop once extended to the public house.

LONDON STREET c. 1915. With the arrival of the motor car came the garages and repair shops, and one local man, Mr. Webber, opened up his business in the High Street, next to famous names such as Liptons, and later Boots the Chemist and Woolworths. Next to Liptons was Mr. Hopkins' shop; the skating rink in the Grand Theatre in Wote Street, now the Haymarket was also owned by him.

LONDON STREET 1988. Looking just as empty as the previous picture, this end of London Street was always quiet compared with the Town Centre end. It is at its busiest at lunch-time when people flock along to the restaurants and food shops. The Red Lion Hotel on the left, is equally busy. Pedestrianised in 1976 the far end of the road now has offices instead of shops.